Original title:
Tropical Starlight

Copyright © 2025 Creative Arts Management OÜ
All rights reserved.

Author: Charles Whitfield
ISBN HARDBACK: 978-1-80581-658-4
ISBN PAPERBACK: 978-1-80581-185-5
ISBN EBOOK: 978-1-80581-658-4

In the Heart of Hazy Tropics

Beneath the moon's bright glow,
A parrot fears to dance,
With rhythm in its feathers,
It trips, oh what a chance!

Lizards laugh in leafy shade,
As coconut falls down,
A monkey snickers from a tree,
Wearing the best frown.

The ocean's waves, a comical sight,
Tickle the toes of fish,
While crabs in tuxedos prance,
Making a dinner wish.

With laughter echoing through the night,
And stars that wink and cheer,
The tropics throw a silly bash,
As friends all gather near.

Lanterned Skies Surrounding the Isles

Underneath a lantern glow,
A pineapple wears a hat,
Swaying to the music,
While a goat sings to the cat.

Fireflies put on a dance,
With lilting steps they swirl,
Ever so slightly tipsy,
In a very glitzy whirl.

Bubbles float like giggles sweet,
While fishes join in play,
Waving fins in silly waves,
In their own fishy way.

The palm trees join the jolly tune,
With fronds that shake and sway,
As laughter spills from every nook,
In a hilarious cabaret.

Under the Gaze of Stars

Beneath the glow of twinkling lights,
The crabs dance funny, giving frights.
A parrot squawks a joke so loud,
While fish make faces, oh so proud.

The moon's a pizza in the sky,
The dolphins leap and say, "Oh my!"
A coconut floats, skipping by,
While laughter echoes, oh so spry.

Silhouettes of a Soothing Sea

At dusk, the shadows play and tease,
Seagulls argue over chips and cheese.
A crab in shades, looking so cool,
While clams debate the latest rule.

The tide giggles with each small wave,
And shells crack jokes, they try to save.
Laughing barnacles start to dance,
While seaweeds sway in a silly prance.

Echoes of the Evening Tide

As waves roll in with a gentle laugh,
A fish tells tales of a narrow path.
A starfish winks, a sly little wink,
While sea cucumbers begin to blink.

The moon spills silver, a joker's grin,
While seashells whisper of secret kin.
Crabby antics, a slapstick show,
As jellyfish float with a graceful flow.

Awakening the Night Bloom

When night unfurls its velvet cloak,
The flowers giggle, oh what a joke!
A bee buzzes with a silly tune,
While frogs croak in the light of the moon.

The trees whisper secrets, giggling low,
As petals dance to a breeze, oh so slow.
An owl hoots, "Hey, don't you see?
We're all just here for the comedy!"

Secret Gardens of the Evening Glow

In secret gardens, chirps abound,
Where frogs wear crowns, and squirrels dance around.
A gopher sings, with a taco in hand,
While fireflies glow like a marching band.

The tulips giggle, the daisies play,
As peacocks strut in a flamboyant way.
A raccoon shapes hats out of random leaves,
While butterflies tickle the dandelions' sleeves.

Radiant Hues of Midnight's Canvas

The moon's a jester, with winks so bright,
Painting the night in colors of delight.
Laughter ripples like waves on a shore,
As kittens crusade in a playful encore.

Stars wear pajamas, their twinkle so grand,
Shooting like arrows, they leap and they stand.
A cat with a cane leads the critters in cheer,
While crickets compose tunes that only they hear.

Dance of the Sea Breeze

The sea breeze giggles, tousling hair,
As surfboards shimmy through salty air.
A jellyfish waltzes with flip-flop flair,
While crabs form a conga, without a care!

Waves crash like laughter on sandy shores,
Seagulls serenade while they steal fish from scores.
Dolphins jump high, in a talent display,
Telling all creatures, 'Come join the fray!'

Night's Veil of Coral Dreams

Coral reefs sparkle like shimmering ice,
As clowns fish crack jokes that are rather nice.
Starfish wear slippers, they shuffle and sway,
In an underwater party, where all come to play.

An octopus juggles while glowing so bright,
Squid paints the currents with colors of light.
With seaweed confetti, the currents partake,
In a coral ballet, make no mistake!

Melodies from the Coral Depths

In the coral depths, fish dance and twirl,
One pink clownfish says, "Look at me whirl!"
A starfish flatly says it's quite the trend,
While bubbles burst, they giggle and blend.

Seahorses boast of their fancy attire,
While the octopus juggles, making them tire.
'Who wears the crown?' the jellyfish glows,
'Um, not me,' says the parrotfish, 'How could it show?'

Celestial Serenade of the Isles

On distant shores, the coconut falls,
While crabs in tuxedos hold fancy balls.
A parrot squawks, 'Hey! Who ate the pie?'
The moon snickers softly, with a twinkling eye.

The palm trees sway, they throw a big bash,
While the beach ball rolls with a playful splash.
A jellybean comet zooms past the sun,
And everyone laughs as they all try to run.

Mystique of the Surf and Sky

Waves whisper secrets, while seagulls complain,
'Why's the ocean salty? Is it from the rain?'
A starfish yawns, 'Come on, take a dive!'
But a crab just waves, 'I'm too cool to jive!'

The surfboards are lined up, in bright colors so bold,
While fish in sunglasses seek out the gold.
A dolphin leaps, making quite the fuss,
Saying, 'Check out my moves, ride this big bus!'

The Soundtrack of Moonlit Reefs

Under the moon, the sandcastles glitter,
As a turtle sings songs, a real crowd-hitter.
A conch shell hums with a vibrant hum,
While everyone dances to the bass and drum.

Starry-eyed hermits in colorful shells,
Wink at the seahorses, who tell silly tales.
'Oh, look at that crab, with his new shiny shoes!'
They all cackle loudly, sharing the news.

Mystical Weavings of Celestial Lullabies

In the jungle where the monkeys swing,
A chorus of frogs begins to sing.
They croak out jokes with glee and cheer,
While fireflies dance, spreading good cheer.

A sloth wearing shades drapes on a tree,
Complaining about the world, oh so carefree.
He chats with a parrot, colorful and bright,
Trading puns till they roll in the night.

Lemurs laugh as they pull silly faces,
Dancing around in playful races.
They spin the tales of the stars above,
While the breeze carries whispers of love.

So gather round, let the fun unfold,
Under the moon, whose light is bold.
The jungle's alive with laughter and flair,
Where every moment shows it truly cares.

Echoes of Distant Worlds and Dreams

Frogs don tuxedos, ready to impress,
On a stage made of leaves, they come to finesse.
The audience—crickets, in their finest attire,
Swinging their wings, igniting the fire.

A raccoon recites lines, with flair and style,
And everyone chuckles, it's been a while.
He claims to be noble, like kings of old,
But rubber duckies crack him up, uncontrolled.

Galaxies swirling, his dreams take flight,
With wishes that tickle, in the starlit night.
As a comet zooms past, it hears him shout,
"Hey wait! Come back, I've got more to tout!"

The moon giggles softly at these strange sights,
While clueless stars join in, lighting the nights.
In cosmic laughter, they drift and play,
Echoing joys that brighten the way.

Luminous Adventure Beneath Winking Stars

A crab in a hat taps its tiny claws,
Dancing around, causing quite the pause.
With every snap, he makes a new friend,
As the waves giggle, they circle and bend.

Starfish juggling shells, a curious sight,
Winking at sea urchins, all filled with delight.
The ocean's a circus, full of bold dreams,
Where fish tell tales of magical streams.

A dolphin scoffs, "I'll beat you at hide,"
While barnacles laugh, stuck to their ride.
Sardines start spinning in a slippery spree,
Making the ocean a place to be free.

Beneath the bright night, adventure calls clear,
With comical antics, there's nothing to fear.
As laughter ripples, life dances ahead,
In a world of delight, let joy spread!

Reflections on a Dreaming Sea

A pelican wears glasses, reading the tide,
It spots little fish, all trying to hide.
With a wink and a quack, it takes to the air,
Announcing in giggles, "Life's not so rare!"

Shells on the shore whisper tales of the past,
As crabs tell their jokes, a comedic blast.
Each wave a giggle, a splash of pure fun,
Under the twilight, adventures run.

A sandcastle stands, with a flag made of kelp,
Defending its territory, all by itself.
With seagulls in armor, they laugh and they play,
Where dreams wash ashore at the end of the day.

So join in the laughter, dance with the breeze,
Let the ocean's heartbeat put your mind at ease.
In these ripples of joy, let's share and declare,
That life is a melody, beyond compare!

The Dance of Light on Gentle Waves

Waves are wiggling like a fish,
Their sparkle makes a silly wish.
Dancing lights with a comical flair,
Jumping fish seem unaware.

Seagulls squawk with laughter in the air,
While crabs do a jig without a care.
Moonlight flickers on the sandy floor,
As ocean whispers beg for more.

Starfish are grooving, don't you see?
The nautical disco, oh what glee!
Turtles spinning in a slow ballet,
All joining in for this grand display.

With each wave crash, the night does smile,
Nature's jesters, full of style.
A melody played by the tides tonight,
Under this wondrous, gleaming light.

Midnight Reveries Under a Canopy of Stars

Stars are winking, having a ball,
A cosmic party, come one, come all.
Crickets chirp in rhythmic tones,
While frogs perform in silly zones.

Clouds drift by on a giant float,
Like fluffy sheep in a starry coat.
Fireflies blink their secret code,
Joining in on this nightly road.

Moonbeams slip through leafy clumps,
Casting shadows that wiggle and jump.
A raccoon giggles with mischievous glee,
As he steals snacks from next to the tree.

Dreams take flight on a breeze tonight,
With silly whispers, they feel so right.
Under the stars, the laughter swells,
In this bright realm where whimsy dwells.

Silhouettes of Paradise in Nightfall

Palms sway, their shadows caper,
With a rhythm like a happy paper.
Laughter echoes through the night,
As crabs participate in moonlit fright.

Coconut drinks spill on the ground,
As we stumble and dance all around.
Pineapples giggle, wearing crowns,
While laughter drowns the sleepy sounds.

Breezy air teases the bright hues,
Tickling our noses like playful news.
A toucan's call, both loud and sweet,
Turns the night into a feathery treat.

Under the palms, with hearts so light,
We sway and twirl until first light.
This paradise, filled with silly cheer,
Reminds us the fun is always near.

Chasing Fireflies in Velvet Nights

Fireflies flicker, little lanterns bright,
Making mischief on this starry night.
We giggle and chase, all in a whirl,
A dance of chaos, oh what a twirl!

In the garden, beneath the gloom,
Flashes of laughter help flowers bloom.
With each little glow, we leap and bound,
In the jolly realm of the night's surround.

Moths join in, with wings that flap,
They chase the sparkles, oh what a trap!
A rabbit hops by, giving a stare,
Wondering what all the laughter's there.

As velvet skies cradle our play,
The fireflies twinkle, leading the way.
In this whimsical chase, we find delight,
In the laughter of stars and the gift of night.

Nights of Enchantment by the Sea

The waves danced like a clown,
With each splash, they fell down.
Crabs jogged, in silly retreats,
As fish giggled, tickling their feet.

Moonlight tossed in playful tricks,
Like shadows doing acrobatic flicks.
Shells whispered secrets to the sand,
While owls wore top hats, oh so grand.

Laughter echoed through the night,
As seagulls staged a flap-fight.
Stars flipped like pancakes in a pan,
While dolphins danced in a funny band.

Together we watched, wide-eyed and bright,
At the comical chaos of the night.
Jellyfish did the limbo with glee,
While starfish grinned, 'Come dance with me!'

Star-Kissed Canopies of Wonder

Under branches of leafy green,
Monkeys threw coconuts, such a scene!
Parrots squawked silly songs at play,
While chameleons danced, changing their way.

A sloth yawned, took a nap on a vine,
Dreaming of ice cream, oh so divine.
Each firefly blinked like a silly light,
As giggles erupted, echoing the night.

Bamboo whispers told jokes in the breeze,
As squirrels laughed, twirling with ease.
The stars above wiggled with glee,
As raccoons held a night tea spree.

Even the moon cracked a smile so wide,
As the jungle boogied, no shame to hide.
In this canopy of joyous delight,
We danced and laughed 'till the morning light.

Heavenly Reflections in the Ocean

The ocean mirrored a face of fun,
Where waves played peek-a-boo, just begun.
Fishes pranced, wearing hats of foam,
While octopuses juggled, feeling at home.

Seaweed swayed in a wiggly dance,
As starfish dressed up for a sea-side romance.
Each splash brought giggles under the sun,
With crabs cracking jokes while on the run.

The horizon painted smiles, oh so bright,
As boats bobbed like corks in pure delight.
Whales sang ballads, hilariously true,
Riding waves, as if they always knew.

Together we laughed till our hearts were free,
Sailing on ships of joy, oh so carefree.
With whirlpools swirling, what a quirky spree,
In this watery world, we found the key!

Secrets of the Moonlit Jungle

In moonlight's glow, the jungle sighed,
Lions wore pajamas, oh what a ride!
Tigers giggled, playing hide and seek,
While parrots squawked, their colors unique.

Bouncing through vines, a monkey slipped,
Landed in puddles with a funny flip.
Crickets chirped in rhythm divine,
As fireflies twinkled like stars on a line.

The shadows whispered, secrets so grand,
As hedgehogs tiptoed, trying to stand.
A waterfall giggled, splashing around,
Echoing laughter through the jungle sound.

Treasures abound in this moonlit maze,
Where laughter blossoms and joy displays.
With the jungle's charm, wild and free,
We danced through the night in joyous decree.

Dreams Beneath the Canopy

In the jungle, the loud frogs croak,
Dreaming of a fancy bespoke cloak.
Monkeys swing with bananas in tow,
While dreaming of disco, oh what a show!

Lizards watch with their big, bulgy eyes,
Wondering when the banana suit flies.
A toucan's laugh fills the warm, balmy night,
As dreams take off in a comical flight.

The shadows dance, and the palm leaves sway,
With the party starting, there's no delay.
Beneath a moon that likes to tease,
The jungle sings with giggles and wheeze.

A sloth wears shades, thinks it's quite fine,
While crickets chirp a blurred-out line.
With dreams like these, who needs sleep?
In this green paradise, the fun runs deep!

Serenade of the Jungle Night

Beneath the stars, the critters pout,
Who left their snack box fully out?
Parrots squawk like they're in a play,
In search of snacks that went astray!

Coconuts in a salsa trance,
While iguanas join the silly dance.
A cacophony of giggles fills the air,
As everyone twirls without a care!

The night is young, the laughter loud,
As jinxed fireflies form a blinking crowd.
Creepy crawlies do a wiggly jig,
Who knew the jungle could be so big?

With each footfall, the fun's begun,
As ants march by, oh what a run!
When critters groove and silly prance,
It's hard not to join the jungle dance!

The Dance of Fireflies

Fireflies glow like stars on a spree,
Trying to outshine a big ol' bee.
They twirl and swirl with gleeful buzz,
As the night sings its whimsical fuzz.

A frog hops by in polka-dot style,
Wondering if he too can compile.
Around him, the glowworms giggle and shine,
Forming a conga line just divine!

Squirrels curl up, rolling their eyes,
Pesky bugs get a surprise, oh my!
The forest chuckles, the palm trees shake,
As fireflies dance, and moments they make!

With each flicker, the laughter spreads,
Even the mushrooms bounce their heads.
In the glow of the night, no one is shy,
Where bugs take flight, and worries fly high!

Mysteries of the Midnight Breeze

At midnight, whispers tickle the air,
As the breeze plays peek-a-boo everywhere.
Chasing shadows, the garden's alive,
With flowers laughing as sirens dive.

Palm fronds wave, joining the spree,
Looking for jokes they can all agree.
An owl roars, thinking he's a star,
Only to find he is not, by far!

Breezes whirl with tales from afar,
Of crickets and nuggets in a candy jar.
Each gust brings giggles, a swirling spree,
In this raucous, riddle-filled jubilee!

As moonlight flickers, they all break free,
Jungle shenanigans dance with glee.
In the midnight tales that twinkle and tease,
A cackle of laughter rides on the breeze!

Glowing Horizons at Sunset's End

The sun dips low, a giant ball,
Painting skies in orange and mauve.
A parrot squawks, 'You missed the call!'
While coconut crabs do the dance they love.

Flip-flops slap on the sandy shore,
Seagulls argue 'bout the best fish fries.
A beach ball rolls, we chase it more,
As sunset giggles, just beneath the skies.

The waves are winking, a cheeky tease,
A jellyfish wobbles, tripping the tide.
While we feast on snacks, oh how they please,
Under a sky where laughter can't hide.

So let's make wishes on bubbles afloat,
And ride the giggles till the stars ignite.
With every splash, we'll sing and gloat,
For fun is best where the day meets night.

Mysteries Beneath the Starry Veil

In the stillness of night, we find a clue,
The crickets chirp in a quirky tune.
A turtle peeks, eyes wide and true,
As fireflies dance, feeling like a goon.

The moon whispers secrets, quite out of line,
While old Mr. Owl calls bingo at dawn.
Raccoons raid snacks, thinking they dine,
Under a sky where the silliness spawns.

Unruly stars giggle in tight little groups,
While a mischievous breeze plays hide and seek.
A lobster in slippers, just one of the troops,
In stories of night, it's laughter we seek.

So grab your goggles, let's make a splash,
In oceans of nonsense where funny things thrive.
With each silly tale, our hearts do clash,
Beneath the bright stars, we're fully alive.

Moonlight's Serenade on Still Waters

A mirror of moonbeams, shiny and bright,
The frogs croak tunes no one understands.
A fish jumps up, what a funny sight,
As ducks quack gossip in their little bands.

The cool breeze teases and wants to play,
While lily pads bob like they're at a show.
A cat sings opera, a nightly ballet,
As shimmering starlight puts on a glow.

Splashing echoes, from a splishy-splash dunk,
A otter does laps, wearing a hat.
In the stillness, we laugh at the funk,
While the moon keeps time, just imagine that!

With every ripple, a giggle does ring,
As crickets support the whimsical stage.
The serenade echoes, let's dance and sing,
In waters that sparkle, there's no need for age.

A Symphony of Shadows and Light

The palm trees sway, in a wacky waltz,
As shadows stretch long, doing disco spins.
A gecko hums, it's not just for faults,
While laughter erupts, where silliness wins.

Beneath the stars, a raccoon does prance,
With mischief wrapped tight 'round its little paws.
A coconut drops, oh what a chance,
To laugh at the derp, it deserves applause!

The tides are composing a cheeky beat,
The moon conducts with a pointy hat.
With each little wave, our hearts skip a beat,
As life dances on, with the fluffiest chat.

So gather your friends, it's time for the night,
Where shadows do jiggle, and smiles are free.
In this wacky symphony of pure delight,
We'll embrace the fun, just you wait and see!

Celestial Canopy

Stars dancing like fireflies,
In a raucous nighttime spree.
The moon chuckles overhead,
Jokes whispered through the trees.

Crickets join in harmony,
Their songs rival a comedy show.
A parakeet laughs so loudly,
Even the shy crabs steal the glow.

The sky paints silly shapes,
With clouds playing dress-up tonight.
A pineapple in a tutu,
Makes us laugh till morning light.

The ocean waves chuckle too,
Bubbling up with playful cheer.
As laughter weaves through the canopy,
A night of joy, so ever clear.

Whispering Palms at Dusk

Palms whisper quite a tale,
As breezes tickle their fronds.
They gossip about the sun,
Who forgot to wear his blonds.

A crab dons oversized shades,
Strutting like he owns the sand.
Every step, a comical move,
In this tropical wonderland.

The sunset giggles at the scene,
As colors clash and swirl around.
Even the dolphins throw a dance,
In a party that knows no bounds.

At dusk, the stars start to plot,
Making wishes like kids at play.
And the palms keep laughing so loud,
Sharing secrets till break of day.

Moonlit Waves and Hidden Shores

Waves shimmer like a disco ball,
Pulsing to the rhythm of the night.
Crabs boogie down on the sand,
While the moon beams down with delight.

Fish make a splashy entrance,
Wearing fins in wild fashion flair.
They flip and flop in the moonlight,
Clearing out the sea for a square.

Seashells gossip on the shore,
Trading tales from years gone by.
A starfish winks at a clam,
In this seaside lullaby.

With laughter echoing all around,
The ocean kisses the land with glee.
Hidden shores become a galas,
Under the moon, wild and free.

Luminous Nights in Paradise

Luminous lights twinkle above,
As critters compete for the best dress.
A flamingo prances by in style,
While a turtle is playing chess.

Mangoes roll down the hill,
As monkeys vie for a taste.
A coconut starts to complain,
"Why am I always last placed?"

The laughter of children fills the air,
As they chase fireflies in shoes too big.
The stars snicker at their antics,
As the gala turns into a jig.

In paradise, the fun never ends,
With joy wrapped in every hug.
Nature's playground shines so bright,
A whimsical night, warm and snug.

A Constellation of Coral Dreams

In the ocean's dance, fish wear hats,
Bubbles make jokes, tickling spats.
Seahorses rave in their stylish suits,
Crabs roll their eyes while dodging the loot.

Jellyfish jive like glittering stars,
Their moves are wild, they don't drive cars.
Octopus giggles, showing eight hands,
While deep-sea turtles form rock bands.

A clam sings opera, it's quite a sight,
Clownfish chuckle, delighting the night.
Lost in the waves, all creatures engage,
Underwater antics, they never age.

Coral castles beam with laughter and cheer,
Dolphins throw parties, it's party time, dear.
So if you dive deep and hear ocean's themes,
Join the fun dance of coral dreams.

Paradise Lost in Midnight's Veil

When bananas wear pajamas, it's quite a scene,
Mangoes play hide and seek, clever and keen.
Coconuts crack jokes, rolling on land,
As palm trees sway, forming a band.

The moon plays maracas, stars strut their stuff,
Under bright lanterns, the air's filled with fluff.
Fruits tango gracefully, dressed to the nines,
While laughter echoes in playful designs.

A parrot squawks puns with a wink and a grin,
While sloths on the sidelines start kicking it in.
Nighttime mischief fills the warm, balmy air,
As everyone stumbles without a care.

So grab a fruit hat, join the wild parade,
In a land where silliness never will fade.
Though paradise shifts under midnight's veil,
We dance 'til the dawn, telling silly tales.

Starlit Veils Over Silent Waters

Reflections shimmer where otters conspire,
With fishy jokes, their giggles won't tire.
A mole in a boat, with snacks packed and neat,
Paddles with laughter, it can't be beat.

A frog in a tux jumps in with a splash,
While turtles in shades take their time and dash.
The fireflies flicker, playing tag in the night,
As crickets compose a symphony of light.

A catfish conducts, with whiskers so grand,
And egrets dance proudly, taking the stand.
Amidst all the chuckles and whimsical sights,
The water flows softly, igniting delights.

Starlit veils drape the water's embrace,
Fish flash their fins, joining the race.
In silent waters, laughter takes flight,
Bringing joy to the depths, a merry respite.

Eternal Whispers of the Night Sky

Balloons float by, with dreams all aglow,
As crabs start a race, putting on quite a show.
The stars pull pranks, give the moon a nudge,
While fireflies play hopscotch, just for the grudge.

A squirrel dons shades, thinking it's cool,
While waves whisper secrets beneath the moon's drool.
The breeze tells tales of the funny and bold,
As creatures concoct mischief, legends retold.

Owls quack in tune, while bats sing in glee,
As raccoons discuss the best spots for tea.
Clouds roll by, puffed and bloated with mirth,
Floating through dreams, they dance for all worth.

So look to the heavens, where laughter ignites,
In eternal whispers, through magical nights.
Join the cosmic gala, where silliness flies,
In the grand scheme of things—the funniest skies.

Glimmering Tides of Paradise

In the night the sea just winks,
A fish with shades it slyly blinks,
The crabs are dancing on the shore,
While surfboards fight for ocean floor.

With cocktails made from bright fruit zest,
The parrots squawk, they're quite the best,
A dolphin jumps, it steals the show,
Then loses crabs to silly flow.

The waves are laughing, can you hear?
They splash our drinks, oh what a cheer!
A sea turtle tries to surf, oh my!
While jellyfish float on by and sigh.

So bring your friends to this delight,
Where every splash is purest light,
The tides will giggle, take your ride,
In glimmering waves, let joy abide!

A Night Beneath Canopied Glow

The moon hangs low, a disco ball,
While geckos dance and have a ball,
The sunbears snore, they're quite the sight,
As stars arrive to join the night.

In this wild fest, the owls hoot loud,
A parrot sings, it's quite the crowd,
With every swing on vines so wide,
The jungle hums, we're filled with pride.

Watch out for vines that trip and tangle,
The monkeys jump, their antics wrangle,
Each leafy laugh, a story told,
Under bright skies, we feel so bold.

So grab your pals, don't miss the fun,
A night of joy for everyone,
With giggles spilling like the dew,
In this wild dream, we're young and true!

Stardust Over the Island Breeze

As laughter stitches through the night,
A coconut rolls, oh what a sight,
The breeze will tickle every tree,
While BBQ smoke sets laughter free.

The sands are warm, a dance parade,
While starfish cheer, their plans well laid,
And fireflies play hide and seek,
With every glow, we leap and squeak.

The waves will crash a silly tune,
As crickets chirp beneath the moon,
A kitefish flies; it's quite the tease,
In stardust dreams, we drift with ease.

So raise a toast with fruity cheer,
To nights of fun and friends that near,
With breezy laughs and sandy toes,
On this bright isle, let joy compose!

Celestial Secrets in the Coconut Grove

Beneath the palms, the secrets swirl,
A monkey sneezes, gives a twirl,
The coconuts gossip in the breeze,
As crabs debate on who will tease.

The owls are plotting their great heist,
To steal a snack, oh that sounds nice,
While iguanas sunbathe with flair,
With every blink, they steal the air.

The fruit bats swoop to join the fun,
Proposing how to outshine the sun,
With every rustle, whispers grow,
In this grove where secrets flow.

So gather 'round, hold tight your drink,
In this wild place, just stop and think,
The laughter blooms beneath the stars,
In coconut dreams, we'll raise our jars!

Lanterns of the Ocean's Heart

Glow of lanterns sways like fish,
They dance in water, make a wish.
Crabs wear hats and twirl around,
While jellyfish swim with no sound.

Seashells gossip, oh what a sight,
Whispers float in the silver night.
Starfish giggle, they can't help it,
As dolphins plan a huge picnic!

A whispering breeze steals the show,
And seaweed parties, oh what a flow.
Mermaids laugh at silly jokes,
While sea cucumbers dance like folks.

Under the moon, we'll share a feast,
With fishy treats, our laughter's increased.
Sipping on sea foam with delight,
Tonight, we bask in ocean's light!

Starry Secrets and Sandy Shores

On sandy shores, secrets we share,
With shovels dancing in the air.
Sand castles wobble, then they fall,
As seagulls chuckle and have a ball.

Starfish sing in off-key tunes,
While crabs are plotting to steal spoons.
Funny shells provide the vibe,
Crafting stories that we describe.

Beneath the stars, we start to slide,
Playing tag with the night tide.
Laughter echoes, oh what a blast,
Under the moon, we forget the past.

Fins and flippers, we leap so high,
Telling tall tales under the sky.
With sand in our shoes, we dance along,
In this playful world where we belong!

A Symphony of Shadows and Light

Under the shade, shadows appear,
Playing tricks, making us cheer.
A monkey plays the bongo drums,
While lizards tap dance, oh, what fun!

Palm trees sway like they're in a show,
As wind whips by with a cheeky blow.
Coconut jokes float in the air,
While turtles ponder without a care.

Lightning bugs flash like bright lights,
Competing with stars for the best sights.
Crickets lead the midnight band,
Rhythmic tunes, so sweet and grand.

With laughter ringing through the night,
We immerse in joy, oh what a delight.
In shadows and light, our spirits play,
A lively dance till break of day!

Beneath the Banyan's Embrace

Underneath our leafy friend,
We share laughter that won't end.
Banyan branches wave goodnight,
As fireflies blink with gentle light.

Squirrels crack jokes about their tails,
While hidden frogs send secret mails.
Whispers ripple through roots below,
Tales of mischief that we all know.

Fragrant flowers join in the cheer,
As hummingbirds buzz, drawing near.
We giggle and swing from the vines,
In this playful world, all is fine.

With shadows dancing, we can't resist,
Creating moments we can't miss.
In the banyan's hug, our dreams ignite,
Together we thrive under starlit night!

Starry Night over Orchard Dreams

In the orchard where bananas sway,
A raccoon steals a pear for play.
Chasing shadows, giggles bloom,
As fireflies light up the gloom.

The moon winks at the dancing trees,
While owls hoot gossip in the breeze.
A squirrel teases, then takes flight,
Who knew fruits could be so bright?

Beneath the stars, the laughter flows,
Each fruit a joke, that rarely shows.
With every bite, the jokes resound,
In every corner of this ground.

So let's toast to the fruity fate,
Where every snack is worth the wait.
We'll laugh, we'll play until it's dawn,
In our dreamland of orchard and fun!

Echoes of the Luminaries' Embrace

The stars are chatty, don't you know?
They gossip freely as they glow.
A comet slips on cosmic ice,
The universe's own buffet price.

Frogs in tuxedos, singing tunes,
With lunar spoons, they dine on moons.
While shooting stars take funny bets,
Who'll get the best of cosmic lets?

In this waltz of absurd delight,
Galaxies dance, oh what a sight!
With playful jests and cosmic spins,
The night wears laughter, it always wins.

So laugh with me, as stardust flows,
Through gardens where the chuckle grows.
Let's celebrate this silly night,
Where echoes of joy take flight!

Ocean's Breath Under Celestial Light

Under the waves, fish wear a grin,
As crabs clap hands, they dance and spin.
A starfish juggles with playful flair,
While dolphins joke, without a care.

Stars above twinkle like fish scales,
As clumsy turtles share their tales.
With seashell hats, they gather near,
In this underwater atmosphere.

The moon's reflection starts to tease,
As jellyfish float with graceful ease.
Laughter bubbles from deep below,
Where ocean's breath steals the show.

Join the fun, don your sea attire,
With waves of humor that inspire.
Let's splash around 'til morning light,
In this sea of joy, pure delight!

Inked Skies and Whispering Dreams

With crayons drawn across the sky,
A flamingo learns to meet a pie.
Underneath the scribbled stars,
Doodles jump in tiny cars.

Clouds become marshmallows sweet,
As dreams take shape on sugar feet.
An octopus paints with flair and grace,
While kittens laugh all over the place.

They hold a party atop a tree,
Where fruit punch flows with glee.
Inked skies shimmer with scribbled fun,
Two Asian elephants become one!

So let's doodle through this night,
With laughter swirling, pure delight.
In worlds of whimsy, we embark,
On whispered dreams that leave a mark!

The Twilight Song of Tropical Blooms

In gardens where the blossoms play,
A feline joins the ballet today.
She twirls among the big, green leaves,
As if they whispered, "Join us, please!"

The daisies giggle as they sway,
While hummingbirds steal nectar away.
An iguana dons a sunhat too,
Claiming it's hard work in the zoo!

The night arrives with its sparkly bling,
Where crickets chirp and the frogs sing.
Underneath the moon's playful glance,
It's animal antics—their evening dance!

So raise a glass of coconut cheer,
To all the weirdos we hold dear.
In twilight's charm, let laughter bloom,
In every corner of this room!

Lanterns of the Night Over Ocean's Edge

The lanterns dangle, swaying wide,
Making waves of colors slide.
A parrot in a sailor's hat,
Sips piña coladas, just like that!

There's a crab who thinks he's a star,
With shades and beads, he drives a car.
He honks at seagulls flying near,
While they squawk, "Boy, you're quite a leer!"

Surfboards stacked, what a mess!
A turtle's trying to impress.
He shimmies like he's got no cares,
While dolphins giggle, calling "Flares!"

So dance beneath the lantern glow,
Where every creature steals the show.
In waves of laughter, splashes bright,
We'll party on until the light!

Empress of the Night Dances with Light

Underneath the shimmering skies,
The empress twirls with giggles and sighs.
Her dress is made of fireflies bright,
Dancing boldly with pure delight!

Monkeys swing, their jokes collide,
While geckos snicker, taking pride.
The moon winks as if in jest,
"Come join the fun—give it your best!"

She leaps with joy, a flip and a spin,
While turtle joins with his serious grin.
"We'll have no frowns, just laughter here,
With every bounce, let's spread the cheer!"

So lavish in the night's embrace,
A wild, happy, nonsensical chase.
With each sharp laugh, the stars take flight,
The empress reigns till morning light!

Secrets Wrapped in Moonlit Magic

Beneath the glow of twilight's grasp,
There's something funny in every clasp.
An octopus wears a shiny crown,
While gossip flows, stirring up the town!

The palm trees sway, they spin and sway,
With raccoons singing, "What a play!"
A crab tap dances, quite a thrill,
While turtles join with a clumsy chill!

The stars sip juice and giggle loud,
While the waves applaud, a cheering crowd.
"Did you hear the tale of the restless seas?
They tickle fish with pancakes and cheese!"

So gather close 'neath the silly night,
Where giggles dance with pure delight.
In secrets wrapped within the gleam,
Let's weave a fun and magical dream!

Ethereal Nightscapes of Enchantment

Under the moon, the crabs do dance,
Waving their claws in a silly prance.
Stars chuckle softly, all aglow,
While a parrot clown tries to steal the show.

The ocean sings with giggles and splashes,
As fish wear wigs, and seaweed mustaches.
Jellyfish float in a bubbly array,
While seahorses trot like they're on display.

A coconut falls with a thud and a bang,
And the hermit crabs laugh, oh how they sang!
Fireflies twinkle, playing hide and seek,
As the palm trees sway, they're the stars of the week.

With winks and whispers from the night sky,
The stars joke around, not shy but spry.
In this enchanted, silly scene,
The night's alive with a laughter routine.

A Tapestry of Nighttime Visions

Balloons floating in a gentle breeze,
Chasing after iguanas and bees.
The lanterns giggle, they flicker and sway,
As the lizards join in the nighttime ballet.

Flamingos strut in their feathered ball gowns,
Sipping on smoothies while wearing small crowns.
Frogs in tuxedos leap from the shore,
A rubber duck race? Oh, we want more!

The moon's got a grin, shining so bright,
While dolphins conduct a symphony of light.
And the night crickets croon in funny tunes,
Just beneath the whimsical swaying dunes.

Stars throw confetti from velvet skies,
As all critters gather, oh what a surprise!
It's a celebration of laughter and cheer,
In this joyous tapestry, nothing to fear!

Fragments of Dreams on Silver Sands

On shimmering shores, where dreams collide,
A crab starts rapping, all full of pride.
Seashells are drummers, keeping the beat,
As fish form a conga line, oh what a treat!

A sandcastle crumbles with a mighty roar,
As a hermit crab calls it "his pantry's door."
Seagulls squawk jokes in a fun little booth,
Selling laughter as currency, that's the truth!

The tide rolls in with a tickle and splash,
While octopuses juggle, and they do it with class.
Starfish cheer loudly, waving their arms,
As the night unfolds with all of its charms.

With every new wave, a chuckle's released,
In this whimsical world, not a moment's ceased.
A symphony of giggles, bright as the moon,
In fragments of dreams, we'll dance till it's noon.

Odes to the Crafted Universe

In the cosmic dance, the planets align,
Each one a character in this grand design.
Saturn—she juggles, while Venus just sings,
As comets fall, sporting glittery wings.

Galaxies swirl, all wearing a grin,
While meteors race, trying to win.
A star boasts loudly, "I'm the brightest tonight!"
But the moon just winks, so subtle and bright.

Asteroids tease with their rocky old jokes,
While space-time giggles with all of its folks.
Neptune pours drinks in his shimmering deck,
While we all float by, just check your speck!

In this crafted universe, laughter's the theme,
Whether sunbeams or stardust, join in the dream.
Let's join this party, cosmic cheer on display,
In odes of hilarity, come dance and sway!

Luminous Breezes and Ember Skies

The breeze tickles my nose, oh what a tease,
A twist of fate, I sneeze with ease.
Fireflies dance in a clumsy parade,
One landed in my drink, how does that taste?

We giggle at clouds, they're fluffy and white,
One hiccuped loudly, caught in the light.
The sun waves goodbye with a wink and a grin,
Now where did I hide that misplaced gin?

Lemons in lemonade, bring on the cheer,
But that lime too sour, bring back the beer!
As laughter ricochets through the cooling skies,
I trip over shadows, oh, what a surprise!

The stars poke fun, with their twinkling blinks,
Telling me secrets, what do they think?
I raise up my cup, a toast to this night,
May we forever dance, under moonbeam light!

Dancing Shadows of Twilight Dreams

In twilight's embrace, shadows begin to dance,
One tripped on a pebble, what a clumsy romance!
They whispered sweet secrets, oh what a tease,
While I'm busy debating my next cheese, please!

A coconut rolled, and it caused quite a scene,
Tangoing on toes, oh it's not so serene.
Palm trees curve, doing the limbo,
I joined in the fun, but fell—oh no!

A star swirled in laughter, at our jitterbug,
Our moves resemble a caffeinated hug.
Each turn a disaster, yet we can't help but cheer,
As we laugh with the night, and dance without fear.

Dreams weave a tapestry, oddly surreal,
A pineapple hat? Now that's a big steal!
With shadows as friends, we twirl till we drop,
When morning arrives, will the fun ever stop?

Moonlit Shores and Coral Hues

At the shore under stars, where the waves like to play,
I found a crab, trying to dance all day.
But with sideways steps, it sworn it could groove,
Yet tripped on its claws, oh, what a move!

Seashells whisper tales, of fish with big dreams,
One wants a top hat, or so it seems.
A dolphin joined in with a splashy design,
It skidded right past—hey, that's my wine!

In moonlight, we gather, with snacks all around,
A feast for the critters, it's joy abound.
I started to dance with a flounder so bold,
But that slippery fellow, would not fit my mold!

So here we all are, on this wild, silly quest,
Finding joy in the dark, we're never at rest.
With giggles and gigawatts, this night is a win,
Let the moonlight keep shining, let the antics begin!

Radiance Over the Lagoon

Above the lagoon, the fireflies ignite,
A chorus of whispers, like laughter in flight.
The frogs are a-singing, it's quite a bizarr,
One croaked out a solo, like a drunken rock star!

The ripples reflect the shimmer and gleam,
Where mermaids are plotting, "Plan a frosty dream?"
I asked for a mermaid, but got a fish instead,
It winked at me slyly, "Crown me king," it said!

Splashing around, I found a way to float,
But all of my giggles? They sank like a boat!
With seaweed on heads, we jest and we joke,
"Next stop, the sea circus!" I declared with a poke.

So here's to the brightness, the fun that we share,
Where laughter and kookiness hang in the air.
In this lagoon of oddities, let's splash and let go,
For life is a party, like a moonlit show!

Nocturnal Echoes in Green Hues

In the jungle, monkeys dance,
Under glowing, leafy trance.
Lizards giggle, frogs sing loud,
While a parrot jests, quite proud.

Fireflies flash a cheeky light,
Never knowing, they take flight.
A sloth questioned his own pace,
Said, "Too slow for this wild race!"

Bright bananas hang with glee,
While chattering bees sip their tea.
Palm trees sway with teasing laughs,
As night drops in like silly giraffes.

Bugs in hats invite a cheer,
While the moon grins, full of beer.
This green world, a humorous sight,
Bathes in the glow of delight.

Starlit Reflections on Water

Ripples giggle, stars play games,
Jumping fish with silly names.
The moon dips low for a peek,
To see the ragged waves cheekily speak.

A frog croaks jokes from the shore,
Making the turtles laugh more.
Splashing ducks in playful rows,
Got not a clue, just strike a pose!

Crickets join with clumsy tunes,
Bouncing under the watchful moons.
Each wave's a chuckle, a little jest,
Even the quiet catfish join the fest.

Rippling dances, water's flow,
Under starlight, they put on a show.
Nature's humor, a playful affair,
As laughter bounces through the air.

The Enchantment of Twilight Whispers

As day slips softly into night,
Fireflies flicker, a funny sight.
Whispers travel 'twixt the trees,
"Did you hear the latest tease?"

The owls hoot in comical tunes,
While raccoons raid the silver spoons.
Laughter echoes through the glade,
As crickets start their evening parade.

Witty winds spin tales so bright,
Filling hearts with sheer delight.
A chameleon grins, wears a new hue,
Saying, "You'll never guess who's who!"

Coconut smiles from the height,
Watching antics in pure delight.
Nature's jesters, all a-scamper,
In the twilight of raucous banter.

Nightfall's Gentle Caress

As darkness drapes its velvet fold,
Laughter echoes, stories told.
The shadows waltz, the stars conspire,
To set the jungle's heart on fire.

A cat with shades demands attention,
While squirrels plot their next prevention.
The nocturnal fun is just begun,
With every tree and every pun.

A walrus shows up at the bay,
Sporting a smile, bright as day.
Banana peels play tricks galore,
As night unveils a comedy tour.

Crickets chirp a witty line,
Under a sky where dreams align.
Every creature plays its role,
In this night of merriment and soul.

Melodies of the Night Cascading Through Palms

The breeze plays tunes on leafy strings,
A chorus sung by little wings.
A pineapple falls, causing a row,
While crabs dance jigs, oh what a show!

Laughter bursts like sparkling fizz,
As everyone forgets what was.
The moon peeks through, taking a sip,
Of coconut drinks, oh what a trip!

Giggling frogs join in the fun,
A party starts with just one pun.
The palmtree sways, a wobbly friend,
Who laughs too hard, its leaves could bend!

So let us dance till dawn's first light,
In the glow of bugs, our hearts feel light.
With silly hats and playful cheer,
We'll sing till morn, let's persevere!

Shadows Embracing the Night's Secrets

Shadows leap like playful sprites,
Chasing dreams on adventurous nights.
A coconut rolls, causing a fuss,
The iguana laughs while making a bus!

The stars giggle, twinkling bright,
As we try to capture a lick of light.
A critter plays hide-and-seek,
Under the moon's soft, silvery streak.

A mischievous breeze pulls at my hair,
Tickling my toes, I can't help but stare.
The shadows whisper secrets so sweet,
About all the snacks to eat with my feet!

With shadows and laughter, we drift and glide,
Together in mischief, we will abide.
Embracing the night with jokes that ascend,
In our cozy realm, we're all just pretend!

A Night's Promise in the Whispering Wind

The wind tickles palms, it whispers low,
Promises of mischief ready to flow.
A firefly boogie lights up the path,
As we join in with our own sweet laugh!

Bananas dance with an evening cheer,
While coconuts giggle, and lend us an ear.
The waves flip-flop, high-fiving the sand,
Creating a party, oh isn't it grand?

A fruit salad flop brings random delight,
As laughter erupts far into the night.
We're pirates of whimsy, lost in our dreams,
With jokes swirling bright as our playful schemes!

Stars poke their heads from behind a cloud,
Cheering us on, they're feeling quite proud.
Together we twirl, under moonlit grace,
In laughter and joy, we find our place!

Opalescent Tides Under Starlight

The ocean giggles, waves splashing bright,
Winking at us, what a marvelous sight!
Glowing seashells tap dance on sand,
While jellyfish float like pals, oh so grand!

The moon's tickling rays make shadows play,
We try to catch them, what a silly fray!
Sandcastles wobble, in jest they stand,
Like proud little kings with their armor unplanned.

Starfish salute with a goofy grin,
As crabs march by, they're ready to win.
The night hums a tune, so carefree and sweet,
Inviting us all to join in the beat!

In this patch of wonder, we twirl with delight,
As opalescent beauty adorns the night.
With laughter as our guide and joy at heart,
We dance under stars, that's just the start!

The Enchanted Lagoon's Embrace

In the lagoon where fish wear hats,
And alligators dance like acrobats,
The water giggles, splashing about,
While frogs recite jokes loud and stout.

With moonlit rays that tickle the palm,
The crickets chirp a ridiculous psalm,
A turtle in shades sips on a drink,
While lizards prance, with no time to think.

The lilies float, wrinkled with glee,
As a beaver brags of the biggest tree,
With every ripple, chaos ensues,
In this lagoon, you can't lose your blues!

So join the party, don't be shy,
With giggling fish and the odd flying pie,
In this magical place of utmost delight,
Where laughter echoes all through the night!

Radiant Echoes of Distant Stars

Stars above wearing shades in the dark,
Twinkling and winking, making their mark,
They play tag with planets, giggle and dive,
Cosmic comedians, the night comes alive!

A comet sneezes, sending a tail,
While meteors tumble, leaving a trail,
They toss about jokes, lighthearted and bright,
Creating bright laughter in the velvet night.

The moon pulls faces, so silly and round,
As starry jesters dance all around,
With aliens chuckling in spaceships nearby,
Making these wonders a comical flyby!

So gaze at the heavens, join in the mirth,
In this galactic hub of joy and rebirth,
Each flash is a chuckle, each shimmer a grin,
In this universe, fun will always win!

Mirage of Light Among the Ferns

Underneath the ferns, there's a giggling breeze,
With fireflies buzzing like zany bees,
They flash their lights in a chaotic dance,
As shadows play tricks that make you prance!

The mushrooms are snickering, all in a bunch,
While critters join in with a joyful crunch,
A rabbit in glasses reads from a book,
Of silly old tales that give quite a hook!

Lizards doing cha-cha up and down the trees,
Drawing turtle crowds that come to tease,
Every rustle, every flick, is a cosmic delight,
In the mirage of giggles that fills up the night.

So step in this world where laughter reigns,
In every glimmer, joy remains,
Amidst the ferns and playful sights,
The mirage of glee ignites our nights!

Celestial Nights and Ocean Sighs

The ocean laughs, bubbling with tease,
As waves frolic and tickle the knees,
Seagulls joke with a flip and a flap,
While crabs write poems in a sandy lap!

Starfish play chess on the warm, golden shore,
While fish in bow ties swim and explore,
A whale tells tales of its wildest dreams,
While jellyfish giggle in swirly streams.

Countless shells echo laughter as they sing,
Chasing crabs that spin in a swing,
The tides know secrets, a playful tease,
In celestial nights that dance in the breeze.

So come join the fun, let your heart glide,
In a world where laughter is the ultimate tide,
With oceanic joy that never is shy,
These celestial nights, oh my, oh my!

Luminary Whispers Among the Leaves

The palms are swaying, what a sight,
With critters dancing in the night.
They whisper secrets to the breeze,
While munching snacks amidst the trees.

A raccoon juggles mangoes too,
While coconut crabs drum a tune.
The fireflies chuckle in their glow,
As sunburned tourists steal the show.

The moonbeams spill like lemonade,
As mischief in the branches played.
Laughter bubbles in the air,
As coyotes join without a care.

Underneath the winking stars,
We laugh at toucans and their cars.
A rally of the night unfolds,
With humor wrapped in marigolds.

Starlit Paths Through Velvet Nights

We tiptoe through the midnight sand,
Where crabs are plotting something grand.
A turtle giggles at our speed,
While parrots squawk, "You'll never lead!"

The silver waves make quirky sounds,
As jellyfish dance in silly rounds.
An octopus with disco lights,
Invites us all to join the sights.

Beneath the glimmers of the sky,
We chase the dreams that leap and fly.
Each footstep leaves a glittery trace,
As shimmers giggle in the race.

Among the stars we find our glee,
Making wishes that are wild and free.
Let's toast with coconuts in hand,
And laugh within this sandy land.

Echoes of the Blushing Horizon

The sun dips low, it's quite a show,
With flamingos in a dance we know.
They prance and wobble, oh what fun,
As laughter bursts before the run.

A parrot roasts the crabs all day,
While sunburned folks start to sway.
The horizon blushes, feeling spry,
As we wave back to a passing pie.

With seaweed hats and sea foam shoes,
We'll strut like stars without a clue.
The dolphins chuckle at our game,
As we all giggle at our shame.

Together we laugh as shadows grow,
And still the laughter starts to flow.
The horizon winks, "Come on, just play!"
With echoes rich and bright all day.

Celestial Bathed Isles

On these islands where dreams collide,
The night's a carnival, come take a ride.
A starfish dons a sailor's hat,
While the seagulls squawk, "What's up with that?"

Coconuts roll and laughing chatters,
As iguanas spin in silly tatters.
The banyan trees whisper, "You're absurd!"
While the nightingale sings a comical word.

It's a gala of colors and joy so bright,
Where the waves and whims form a pure delight.
With every sunset, laughter unfurls,
As we dance and twirl in this sea of pearls.

A comet zips, a silly tease,
And everyone joins, as they please.
So let's raise a cheer to these beautiful sights,
Where laughter reigns and fun ignites.

www.ingramcontent.com/pod-product-compliance
Lightning Source LLC
Chambersburg PA
CBHW072131070526
44585CB00016B/1634